WE'RE GOING ON A BOOK HUNT

Pat Miller
Pictures by Nadine Bernard Westcott

Fort Atkinson, Wisconsin
www.upstartbooks.com

For Chris, Marty, and Bonnie—
and reading till the streetlights come on.
—P. M.

To Nola and Margo.
—N. B. W.

Published by UpstartBooks
W5527 State Road 106
P.O. Box 800
Fort Atkinson, Wisconsin 53538-0800
1-800-448-4887

Text © 2008 by Pat Miller
Illustrations © 2008 by Nadine Bernard Westcott

We're going on a book hunt.

We're going to find a good one.

We know how.

Not too easy,

Not too hard,

But just right.

Here it is—the library.
Can't scream or run about,
Can't skip or yell and shout.
We'll have to be considerate.

Tip toe, tip toe, tip toe.

Here it is—the shelf marker.
Can't look without it.
Shows where the book fits.
We'll have to slide the marker in.

Slippy slide, slippy slide, slippy slide.

We're going on a book hunt.
We're going to find a good one.

We know how.

Not too easy,

Not too hard,

But just right.

Here it is—a book.
Can't tell from outside.
Have to look inside.
We have to see what size it is.

Peek and turn, peek and turn, peek and turn.

We're going on a book hunt.
We're going to find a good one.

We know how.

Not too easy,

Not too hard,

But just right.

Here it is—the choosing part.
Can't read a hard one.
Don't want an easy one.
We'll have to count our fingers.

Miss a word, finger up.
Stop at five.

Here it is—the perfect book.
Can't be rough with it.
Can't be tough with it.
We'll have to treat it kindly.

Cross and hug, cross and hug,
cross and hug.

We're going on a book hunt.
We're going to find a good one.
We know how.
Not too easy,
Not too hard,
But just right.

Here it is—the book check.
Can't keep it always.
Can keep it two weeks.
We'll have to bring our book back.

Beep boop beep, beep boop beep, beep boop beep.

We're going on a book hunt.
We're going to find a good one.

We know how.
Not too easy,
Not too hard,
But just right.

Here we are—back in class.
Can't wait to read the words.
Can share it with our friends.

We'll have to turn carefully.

At the corner, corner, corner.

Here we are—our books are done.
Time to take our books back.
Time to choose some other ones.

Return
library
books
today.

Tip toe, tip toe, tip toe.

Slippy slide, slippy slide, slippy slide.

Peek and turn, peek and turn, peek and turn.

Miss a word, finger up. Stop at five.

Cross and hug, cross and hug, cross and hug.

Beep boop beep, beep boop beep, beep boop beep.

At the corner, corner, corner.

We're going on a book hunt.
We're going to find a good one.
We know how.
Not too easy,
Not too hard,
But just right.